Majisty's

Mime Made Easy
RELOADED

The truth about Christian Mime!

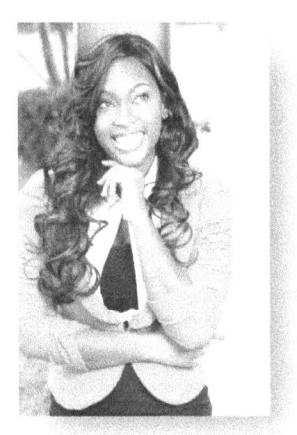

Majisty E. Dennis

Majisty's

Mime Made

Easy

RELOADED

The truth about Christian
Mime!

By Mime Expert &
Extraordinaire

Majisty E. Dennis

Table of Contents

Dedication

First, I dedicate this book to God my heavenly father. Thank you Father for this revelation and insight you have given me.

Secondly, I dedicate this book to everyone who ministers through mime. I pray that the information in this book strengthens the foundation of your ministry like it has mine!

Chapter 1

What is Mime?

Mime: To act out; represent, copy, imitate or to mirror. To tell a story; without talking, using only one's facial expressions, body movements, and hand gestures.

The art of mime primarily focuses on using gestures, movements, and facial expressions. It is an art form in which people act out real life scenarios and portray characters in silence.

Mime as we know it today was introduced to America as an entertaining form of theater. The purpose of mime be it in the secular or spiritual arena is to give a visual presentation of a story.

Mime presentations can be choreographed to music, sounds, sermons, literature, or even silence! You can tell any story you want when you mime!

Christian Mime

Since 1981, Christian churches around the world have started including mime ministry presentations in their worship services. During worship services people will act out lyrics to music with a scriptural theme. All while combining pantomime movements with various styles of dance as an expression of worship to God and encouragement to the congregation.

 As we continue through this text we will refer to Christian Mime as 'the mime ministry'. A person who participates in the mime ministry is considered a 'mime minister'. *Christian Mime is the word of God being brought to life through motion!*

The biblical purpose of Christian Mime is to edify people and prophecy God's word from the scriptures using our bodies to do so. As mime ministers we should remember that the Word always comes first. The bible tells us in *John 1:1 In the beginning was the Word, and the Word was with God, and the Word was God (NKJV).* John 1:1 shows us the preeminence of the word of God and how critical God's word is to everything around us. When we mime, every aspect of our presentation should expose the word of God in a creative way.

Arsenal Check

Fill in the blank.

1. Christian Mime is the _____ of God being brought to life through motion!

2. As mime ministers we should remember that the _____ always comes first.

Circle 'True' or 'False' for each statement.

3. When we mime, every aspect of our presentation should expose the word of God in a creative way.
True or False

Circle the correct answer.

4. A person who participates in the mime ministry is considered a _____.

    a. Mime minister b. Dancer

Arsenal Check: Answers

Fill in the blank.

1. Christian Mime is the <u>word</u> of God being brought to life through motion!
2. As mime ministers we should remember that the <u>word</u> always comes first.

Circle 'True' or 'False' for each statement.

3. When we mime, every aspect of our presentation should expose the word of God in a creative way. *True*

Circle the correct answer.

4. A person who participates in the mime ministry is considered a

_____.

   a. Mime minister

Chapter 2
The First Mime

Mime as Prophecy

The prophet Ezekiel is a great example of someone who acted out a prophecy from the Lord. Let's take a look at the following passage concerning the siege of Jerusalem. *Ezekiel 4:1-4 "You also, son of man, take a clay tablet and lay it before you, and portray on it a city, Jerusalem. 2 "Lay siege against it, build a siege wall against it, and heap up a mound against it; set camps against it also, and place battering rams against it all around. 3 "Moreover take for yourself an iron plate and set it as an iron wall between you and the city. Set your face against it, and it shall be besieged, and you shall lay siege against it. **This will be a sign to the house of Israel.** 4 "Lie also on your left side, and lay the iniquity of the hose of Israel upon it. According to the* *number of the days that you lie on it, you shall bear their* iniquity*.*

God was not pleased with the people of Jerusalem and had plans to punish them. God gave Ezekiel a special set of instructions that we see highlighted line by line in Ezekiel chapter four that describe the siege of Jerusalem.

When God is trying to get us to understand something He will move through any means necessary; including visual art.

 Ezekiel performed one of the first mimes in the bible. He showed us how to prophesy with our body!

In Christian Mime, be it a song, sermonette, or pantomime; the foundation of mime is based on the word of God. As mime ministers, we have a prophetic anointing and a prophetic assignment that allows us to create a visual demonstration of what God is saying for the time and season. **Mime is a prophetic anointing!**

Prophecy is declaring God's plans and intentions for the future. When God gives us a prophecy it is an opportunity to partner with Jesus Christ to see the will of God done in the earth. Prophecy is a primary function and expression of the prophet. To prophecy is to express the word of God. Mime is one way to express prophecy.

In the ministry of mime, it is critical to understand the correlation between the Word of God, prophecy, and the art of mime.

Desire to Prophesy! Desire to Mime!

1 Corinthians 14:1, 3-4: (1) Pursue love, and desire spiritual gifts, but especially that you may prophesy. (3) But he who prophesies speaks edification and exhortation and comfort to men. (4) He who speaks in a tongue edifies himself, but he who prophesies edifies the church (NKJV).

Let's take a closer look at the meaning of some of the key words in this scripture.

Edify: to instruct or benefit, especially morally or spiritually; uplift

Exhort: urge, advise, or caution earnestly, admonish urgently

Comfort: to soothe console, or reassure; bring cheer to relief in affliction; consolation; solace

1 Corinthians 14:1, 3-4 tells us that prophecy:

1. Brings edification to men.
2. Brings exhortation to men.
3. Brings comfort to men.
4. Edifies the church.

Because *mime is a way we illustrate prophecy*; we understand that the prophetic ministry of mime also:

- Brings edification to men.
- Brings exhortation to men.
- Brings comfort to men.
- Edifies the church.

The mime ministry is meant for the edification of the Body of Christ. This explains why people are often deeply moved within their souls and spiritually built up when they see the mime ministry.

Notice that the scripture tells us that prophecy can apply to all men; even those not in the church. Some mime ministers may be called to prophesy through mime in other areas of society.

Others may extend their mime ministry to afterschool programs, homeless shelters, or local community centers.

Now let's take a look at *Acts 2:17-18:* *'And it shall come to pass in the last days, says God, That I will pour out of My Spirit on all flesh; Your sons and your daughters shall prophesy, Your young men shall see visions. Your old men shall dream dreams. (18) And on My menservants and on My maidservants I will pour out My Spirit in those days; and they shall prophesy.* (NKJV)

We are living in the last days and God is fulfilling His promise to pour out His spirit on all flesh! No wonder we have seen such an increase in those who desire to mime! Embrace the outpouring of God's spirit to prophesy through mime!

Arsenal Check

Fill in the blank

1. Prophecy brings _____, and _____ to men.
2. We are living in the _____ days.

Circle 'True' or 'False' for each statement

3. Mime is a way we illustrate prophecy. *True or False*

4. People can extend their mime ministry to other areas of society. *True or False*

Circle the correct answer

5. Who is the prophet that showed us the first mime in the Bible?
   a. Abraham
   b. Ezekiel
   c. Daniel

Arsenal Check: Answers

Fill in the blank

1. Prophecy brings <u>edification</u>, <u>exhortation</u>, and <u>comfort</u> to men.

2. We are living in the <u>last</u> days.

Circle 'True' or 'False' for each statement

3. Mime is a way we illustrate prophecy.

   True

4. People can extend their mime ministry to other areas of society.
   True

Circle the correct answer

5. Who is the prophet that showed us the first mime in the Bible?
   b. Ezekiel

Chapter 3
Imitators of Christ

Little "Copycats"

Genesis 1:27: So God created man in His own image; in the image of God He created him; male and female He created them (NKJV). This Scripture tells us that when God created us He intended us to be a miniature model of Him. Our lives should be a reflection God's character that He showed us through Jesus Christ. In essence, we are little copycats of Christ.

The same concept applies to our mime choreography. When we mime, our objective should be to imitate or portray an aspect of life's circumstances and demonstrate how God can fix situations we may face in lives.

Imitators of Christ

Ephesians 5: 1-2: Therefore be imitators of God as dear children.(2) And walk in love, as Christ also has loved us and given Himself for us, an offering and a sacrifice to God for a sweet –smelling aroma (NKJV).

The objective of mime choreography should be to use our craft to physically demonstrate a reflection of God's characteristics. With this in mind, mime can be used as the ministry it was designed by God to be and lives will be changed around the world.

Arsenal Check

Fill in the blank

1. In essence, we are little _____ of _____.

2. Ephesians 5:1 Therefore be imitators of God as dear _____.

Circle 'True' or 'False' for each statement.

3. The objective of mime should be to use our craft to physically demonstrate a reflection of God's characteristics.
   True or False

Circle the correct answers.

4. Ephesian 5:1-2 instructs us to be
   a. The best we can be
   b. Happy
   c. Imitators of God as dear children

Arsenal Check: Answers

Fill in the blank

1. In essence, we are little <u>copycats</u> of <u>Christ</u>.
2. Ephesians 5:1 Therefore be imitators of God as dear <u>children</u>.

Circle 'True' or 'False' for each statement.

3. The objective of mime should be to use our craft to physically demonstrate a reflection of God's characteristics.
   True

Circle the correct answers.

4. Ephesian 5:1-2 instructs us to be
   c. Imitators of God as dear children

Chapter 4

Foundational Scriptures for Mime

When asked typical questions like "Where is mime in the bible?" Every mime should have a few passages from the Bible committed to memory, knowing both chapter and verse.

"Why is it important to memorize foundational scriptures about mime?" Well, I'm glad you asked. Many people, who do not mime, will ask for biblical text on the mime ministry because they genuinely want to know. Failure to give curious people a specific answer when they are seeking truth:

1. Causes you not to look knowledgeable about an area that you are called to.
2. Could cause the person who is asking to reject the prophetic ministry of mime as a whole.

Keep these scriptures in mind to help you carry out the true purpose of the ministry of mime:

- Ephesians 5:1-2 Therefore be imitators of God as dear children. (2) And walk to love, as Christ also has loved us and given Himself for us, an offering and a sacrifice to God for a sweet-smelling aroma. (KJV)
- Psalm 150:4: Praise Him with the timbrel and dance; Praise Him with stringed instruments and flutes! (KJV)
- Acts 2:17: 'And it shall come to pass in the last days, says God, That I will pour out of My Spirit on all flesh; Your sons and your daughters shall prophesy, Your young men shall see visions. Your old men shall dream dreams.

- John 1:1: In the beginning was the Word, and the Word was with God, and the Word was God (NKJV).
- Ezekiel 4:1-4 (1) "You also, son of man, take a clay tablet and lay it before you, and portray on it a city, Jerusalem. (2) "Lay siege against it, build a siege wall against it, and heap up a mound against it; set camps against it also, and place battering rams against it all around. (3) "Moreover take for yourself an iron plate and set it as an iron wall between you and the city. Set your face against it, and it shall be besieged, and you shall lay siege against it. **This will be a sign to the house of Israel.** (4) "Lie also on your left side, and lay the iniquity of the hose of Israel upon it. According to the number of the days that you lie on it, you shall bear their iniquity.

Arsenal Check

Fill in the blank

1. Every mime should have a few passages from the Bible committed to memory knowing both _____ and _____.

2. People ask for _____text on mime because they genuinely want to know.

Circle 'True' or 'False' for each statement.

3. Ezekiel's act was not a sign to the house of Israel. *True or False*

Circle the correct answers.

4. Which of the following is *not* a key scripture for mime?
    a. Ezekiel 4:1-4
    b. John 1:1
    c. Genesis 100:10
    d. Ephesians 5:1-2

Arsenal Check: Answers

Fill in the blank

1. Every mime should have a few passages from the Bible committed to memory knowing both chapter and verse.
2. People ask for biblical text on mime because they genuinely want to know.

Circle 'True' or 'False' for each statement.

3. Ezekiel's act was not a sign to the house of Israel. *False*

Circle the correct answers.

4. Which of the following is *not* a key scripture for mime?
   c. Genesis 100:10

Chapter 5

Mime Takes the Stage

Mime Takes the Stage

In Athens, Greece masked actors would perform outdoors, in daylight before audiences of 10,000 or more during festivals to honor Dionysus, the Greek god of theater.

Today, we use gospel mime in the church because we understand this key principle: **God did not give Satan the authority to create anything**. Satan may have power but his authority is limited!

Let's take a look at authority and power!

Authority: a power or right delegated or given; authorization

Power: ability to do or act; capability of doing or accomplishing something

We see an excellent example of God limiting Satan's authority when it comes to the trying of God's servant Job. *Job 1:12 And the Lord said to Satan, "Behold, all that he has is in your power; only do not lay a hand on his person." So Satan went out from the presence of the Lord.* (NKJV) God allowed Satan to 'try' everything regarding Job but would not let him take Job's life.

Mime belongs to God and was created by Him to be a prophetic ministry. Satan cannot create; he can only copy what God does. When God makes something good the devil will always try to make a copy of it that is evil and perverse. *Everything the devil does is counterfeit or a fake copy of what God did.* The devil tried to pervert mime into being used in vain instead of it being an act of worship to the one true God Elohim and the ministry-tool that it that God created it to be!

Satan does not have more power and authority than God. Now that we know God did not give Satan the authority to create; we can understand that Satan did not create mime. God did!

#CreativeMinds

God is the one and only creator. God, our father, gave us His creative mind to glorify Himself. That is what allows us to be creative! Mime is a gift to the church to express the word so people can understand it clearly! **Our choreography should be a unique expression of who we are given in surrender to God. Creativity is the opportunity to express your God-like nature.** God made special room for the gift of mime in the church!

Arsenal Check

Fill in the blank.

1. Satan does _____ have more and authority than God.
2. Creativity is the _____ to express your God-like nature.

Circle 'True' or 'False' for each statement.

3. God is the one and only creator. *True or False*
4. Having God as our father allows us to be creative. *True or False*

Circle the correct answer.

5. Who created mime?
   a. God
   b. Satan
   c. Ezekiel

Arsenal Check: Answers

Fill in the blank.

1. Satan does <u>not</u> have more and authority than God.
2. Creativity is the <u>opportunity</u> to express your God-like nature.

Circle 'True' or 'False' for each statement.

3. God is the one and only creator. *True*
4. Having God as our father allows us to be creative. *True*

Circle the correct answer.

5. Who created mime?
   a. God

Chapter 6

Genres of Mime

There are many categories of film and literature. The categories, better known as genres, include romance, action, horror, science-fiction, documentaries, and comedies to name a few. Just like there are many genres of books and movies, there are also different genres of mime.

Every genre of mime falls under the following two categories of mime:

1. Literal mime
2. Abstract mime

Literal mime is an exact depiction of events while abstract mime focuses on an emotional interpretation of the scenario.

Consider the comparison between the two major categories of mime:

1. Literal Mime
   - Primarily used for exact messages, comedy and theater
   - Generally tells a story with a conflict through the use of a main character
   - The actions and visual design clearly tell the viewers the story which is often humorous

2. Abstract Mime
   - Used to generate an emotional response, feelings, thoughts and images about a serious topic or issue.
   - Typically, there is no plot or central character
   - Considered a more intuitive experience.

Let's take a look at specific genres of mime within each category of mime.

Clowning

Clowning appeared shortly after World War II, when Marcel Marceau, also known as Bip the Clown, came on the scene. Both pantomime and clowning became more popular around 1947. It became more frequent amongst people in the United States from 1955-2000.

Gospel Mime

Gospel Mime also referred to as Christian Mime, includes a combination of mime and dance. Gospel mime features pantomime, prophetic acts, dramatic interpretive movement, dance, and facial choreographed to the words of inspirational songs, messages, and scriptures. Gospel mime appeared in the United States in 1981. It is one of the newest genres of mime.

Mime Sign

There is a genre of mime that uses sign language as well as pantomime movements. It was created by a man name Bernard Bragg who studied under Marcel Marceau in Paris in the 1950s. Bernard Bragg was born deaf into a deaf family which may have been a source of inspiration for his unique spin on mime.

Mime is not to be confused with:

- Praise dance
- Hip-hop
- Liturgical dance
- Pop-locking
- Krump dancing

While new forms of mime and artists' personal style incorporate these dance styles; neither of those forms are the foundation of the art.

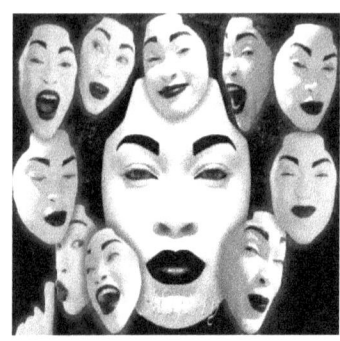

Why the Face?

Facial expressions are an essential part of any genre of mime that cannot be neglected. While attempting to use mime to create a literal scene; the mime artist must use facial expressions so the audience sees the reality of their scene. When a person is portraying abstract or gospel mime they must be able to demonstrate the emotions of the storyline and characters on their face. Facial expressions are equally as important as body movements.

Arsenal Check

Fill in the blank.

1. The mime sign genre was created by a deaf man named _____ _____.

2. Facial _____ are _____ as important as body movements.

Circle 'True' or 'False' for each statement.

3. Clowning appeared shortly before World War II. *True or False.*

4. There are two major categories of mime. *True or False*

Circle the correct answer.

5. Which of the following is not one of the two major categories of mime?
   a. Praise Dance
   b. Literal Mime
   c. Abstract Mime

Arsenal Check: Answers

Fill in the blank.

1. The mime sign genre was created by a deaf man named <u>Bernard Bragg</u>.
2. Facial <u>expressions</u> are <u>equally</u> as important as body movements.

Circle 'True' or 'False' for each statement.

3. Clowning appeared shortly before World War II. *False*.
4. There are two major categories of mime. *True*

Circle the correct answer.

5. Which of the following is *not* one of the two major categories of mime?
   a. Praise Dance

UNLOCKED! RE-LOADED!

God left many gifts to the body of Christ, the mime ministry being one of them. Becoming informed and knowledgeable about your God-given assignment will unlock explosive ministry potential! Regardless of your level of mime experience; keeping the weapons of this text in your arsenal will keep you unlocked and reloaded for your new season!

Declare this for your ministry:

- My mime will be used as worship to declare and make known the greatness of God!
- God's message is clear in my choreography!
- I am equipped with the knowledge I need to be effective!
- I am unlocked and reloaded in Jesus Name!

Paint Exclusive

One of the primary distinguishing factors of a mime is their face paint. Mimes should use white face paint as a base with black contrast. The purpose of wearing mime make-up is to bring attention to the facial expressions. It is a theater technique that uses contrasting shades to make facial expressions highly visible from far away.

Below is a list of the mime supplies I use on myself and my students!

1. Kryolan SupraColor Clown White Makeup
2. Mehron Pro-Pencil Slim (Black)
3. Mehron Pro-Pencil Jumbo (Absolutely Black)
4. Mehron Pro-Pencil Slim (White)
5. White Eyeshadow Base

6. Ben Nye Dual Hole Pencil Sharpener
7. White Make Up Wedges
8. 'Very Black' Mascara
9. Huggies Baby Wipes
10.   Vaseline

Notes

Notes

Notes

About *Majisty* Ministries

Majisty Ministries reaches three areas: **Mime, Ministry, and Motivation.**

Majisty Mime Ministry
Majisty brings fourteen years of experience in teaching the gift, art, and skill of mime. She teaches both young and old in the community and abroad through classes, workshops, books, and conferences.

Ministry
Majisty has a God-given passion to see revival in the earth. She travels as a prophet ministering the word of God!

Motivation
Having launched her first company at the age of fifteen years old; Majisty shares her entrepreneurial experience with young ladies and encourages them to pursue their dreams. While sharing her faith, Majisty aims to inspire young girls to abstinence until marriage. Majisty is passionate about seeing her generation reach their full potential!

To bring Mime Expert and Extraordinaire, Majisty, to a city near you; email us at majistyministries@gmail.com

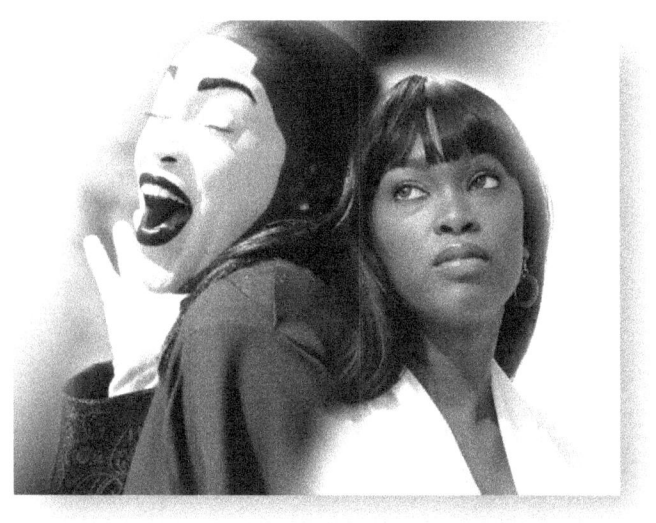

Majisty

Credits

www.dictionary.com

Xcellence Photography

Jpeg Photography